# N IN
# SPORTS MEDIA

BY HEATHER RULE

**SportsZone**

An Imprint of Abdo Publishing
abdopublishing.com

**abdopublishing.com**

Published by Abdo Publishing, a division of ABDO, PO Box 398166, Minneapolis, Minnesota 55439. Copyright © 2018 by Abdo Consulting Group, Inc. International copyrights reserved in all countries. No part of this book may be reproduced in any form without written permission from the publisher. SportsZone™ is a trademark and logo of Abdo Publishing.

Printed in the United States of America, North Mankato, Minnesota
042017
092017

THIS BOOK CONTAINS
RECYCLED MATERIALS

Cover Photo: Paul Spinelli/AP Images
Interior Photos: Paul Spinelli/AP Images, 1, 25; Greg Nelson/Sports Illustrated/Getty Images, 4–5; AP Images, 6, 17; Gayle Shomer/KRT/Newscom, 8; Scott Boehm/AP Images, 11; RFS/AP Images, 12; Michael Zagaris/Getty Images Sport/Getty Images, 14–15; Dave Pickoff/AP Images, 19; PBL/AP Images, 20; Matthew Stockman/Getty Images Sport/ Getty Images, 23; Suzanne Vlamis/AP Images, 27; Lennox McLendon/AP Images, 28; Reed Saxon/AP Images, 31; Steve Senne/AP Images, 33; Ray Carlin/Icon Sportswire BAR/ Newscom, 34; Bill Kostroun/AP Images, 36; Tom Maguire/Big East Conference/Collegiate Images/Getty Images, 38–39; George Gojkovich/Getty Images Sport/Getty Images, 40; Duncan Williams/Cal Sport Media/Newscom, 42–43; Image of Sport Image of Sport Photos/Newscom, 44

Editor: Patrick Donnelly
Series Designer: Laura Polzin
Content Consultant: Rita Liberti, PhD, Professor of Kinesiology, California State
    University, East Bay

**Publisher's Cataloging-in-Publication Data**

Names: Rule, Heather, author.
Title: Women in sports media / by Heather Rule.
Description: Minneapolis, MN : Abdo Publishing, 2018. | Series: Women in
    sports | Includes bibliographical references and index.
Identifiers: LCCN 2017930237 | ISBN 9781532111587 (lib. bdg.) |
    ISBN 9781680789430 (ebook)
Subjects: LCSH: Sports media--Juvenile literature. | Women in professions--
    Juvenile literature. | Communication in sports--Juvenile literature.
Classification: DDC 070--dc23
LC record available at http://lccn.loc.gov/2017930237

# TABLE OF
# CONTENTS

# PIONEERS AND TRAILBLAZERS

The clock is winding down. The newspaper editor wants the reporter to get reactions from players and coaches after the game. The other reporters stream into the locker room when the game ends. But one of them is stopped at the door. This reporter can't go inside because she's a woman.

Sounds crazy, doesn't it? Today's sports media is filled with women in key roles at all levels, from editing and writing to reporting and producing television broadcasts. But that wasn't always the case. It wasn't so long ago that women were outsiders in the media world, clearing hurdles and fighting battles their male counterparts never dreamed of facing.

Female sports journalists have been around for more than a century, even if there were not very many of them at first. Judith Cary Waller,

It's no longer unusual for a woman to be a sports reporter. But that wasn't always the case.

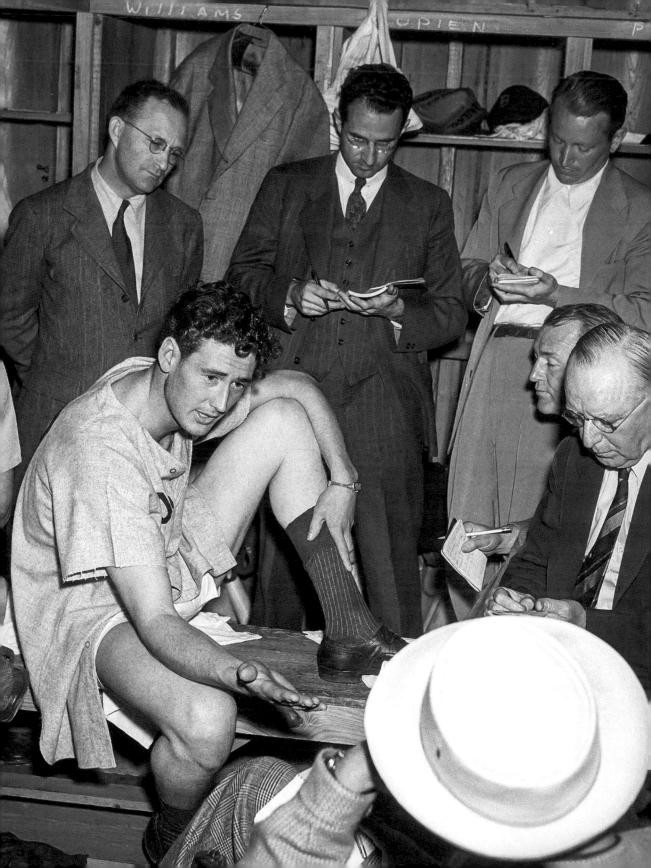

known as the "First Lady of Radio," started her broadcast career in 1922 when she was hired to run the radio station WGU (later known as WMAQ) in Chicago. She was the first station manager of the city's second-ever radio station.

Waller produced the first play-by-play radio broadcast of a college football game in 1924 when the University of Chicago beat Brown University 19–7. Then she pursued the idea of putting Major League Baseball (MLB) games on the air, too. Chicago Cubs home games were broadcast on WMAQ starting in 1926.

During World War II (1939–1945), a shift took place in the workforce. Before the war, it wasn't common for women to work outside the home. But with men serving in the armed forces, many women began taking their place to keep the country running.

During this time, Mary Garber launched her sports journalism career in Winston-Salem, North Carolina. She filled in for the sports editor of the *Twin City Sentinel* when he joined the US Navy in 1944. Covering sports was a man's world, so Garber often had to sit with players' wives in the crowd instead of in the press box. She faced

Baseball legend Ted Williams meets with a group of reporters—all male—in the Boston Red Sox locker room in 1942.

Mary Garber puts the finishing touches on a story in 1998. She was still reporting on high school sports at the age of 82.

other challenges, too. Garber was banned from the locker rooms, treated differently by coaches and players, and often ignored by other sports writers.

# MIDY MORGAN

Maria "Midy" Morgan was considered the first female sportswriter. She covered horse racing for *The New York Times* starting in 1869. Morgan moved to New York from Ireland and took the only job available at the paper: livestock reporter. It was a good fit, as she had grown up around horses. Morgan spent 23 years covering the livestock market news, horse racing, and dog and cat shows. Of course, Morgan was a rare exception. It would be decades before other female sports reporters joined the field.

But Garber stuck with it and became a true pioneer among female sports journalists. In 2005, she was the first woman to receive the *Associated Press* Sports Editors' Red Smith Award for major contributions to sports journalism. As she accepted the award, Garber reflected on her impact on the industry: "I hope some little girl out there knows now that she can be a sportswriter if she wants to be."

Then there's Lawrie Mifflin, the first female sports reporter at the *New York Daily News*. Her big break came at the 1976 Summer Olympics when the *Daily News* sent her to Montreal, Canada, to cover gymnastics, women's track and field, and swimming and diving. Mifflin went on to cover the New York Rangers of the National Hockey League (NHL) for the *Daily News*.

Gayle Gardner was another trailblazer for female sports journalists. Gardner was a sportscaster at WJZ in Baltimore in the early 1980s. It was a time when women didn't often get the chance to advance their careers at a local level. Working at smaller TV stations or newspapers gives reporters a chance to sharpen their skills early in their careers. Many women had to break through in a major market or not at all.

Veteran broadcaster Jim Simpson recommended Gardner to ESPN. Gardner took that opportunity and ran with it. She worked at ESPN from 1983 to 1987, hosting the network's flagship highlight show *SportsCenter* among other duties. Gardner moved

**Jane Chastain was the first woman to broadcast live sports over network television. She was part of the team that called NFL games for CBS in 1974. She later hosted radio shows called "Football for Women" and "The Jane Chastain Show—Everything You've Always Wanted to Know About Sports But Were Afraid to Ask."**

Even the press box was once off-limits for women, but it's become a much more welcoming place for female reporters over the years.

on to NBC as a features reporter for its National Football League (NFL) pregame and halftime coverage.

There weren't many barriers that Gardner didn't break through. In 1993 she became the first woman to provide

play-by-play for a televised MLB game when she called the Cincinnati Reds versus the Colorado Rockies for KWGN-TV in Denver. This milestone paved the way for future play-by-play broadcasters such as Doris Burke and Pam Ward.

These women opened the door for female sports journalists with plenty of "firsts." They broke into a field that was formerly dominated by men. The next step: crossing over into the locker room.

Female reporters were granted access to men's locker rooms for the first time in 1978.

# ONCE A MAN'S WORLD

One of the biggest hurdles for female sports journalists was gaining access to locker rooms and press boxes. Sports journalists need access to these areas when they're covering games. Interviewing players and coaches after games is a crucial part of the job.

Throughout the 1960s and 1970s, women were commonly denied that access. Some female sports reporters found ways to work around it. Betty Cuniberti was the first female sportswriter in the Los Angeles Dodgers press box and the first female sports reporter at the *San Francisco Chronicle*. Cuniberti couldn't get into locker rooms, so she found other ways to get interviews. She asked legendary Ohio State University football coach Woody Hayes to join her on a ride at Disneyland just so they could talk. It wasn't fair that she didn't have the same access her male colleagues had, but Cuniberti didn't want to complain. She wanted to prove that she could do the job anyway.

Betty Cuniberti interviews a member of the Oakland Raiders in the hallway outside the team's locker room.

Robin Herman was another reporter who helped break the locker-room barrier. In the early 1970s she was the first full-time female *New York Times* sports reporter. Herman covered the NHL and specifically the New York Rangers beat. But she wasn't allowed to interview players in the locker room. Instead she had to meet with them in the hallway outside the room.

Finally two coaches at the 1975 NHL All-Star Game unexpectedly allowed Herman and radio reporter Marcel St. Cyr into the locker room. They're believed to be the first female media members to set foot in a men's professional sports locker room.

Anne Doyle was one of the first women hired as a television sports anchor and reporter for a major-market station. She worked at the CBS station in Detroit from the mid-1970s until 1983. Doyle initially encountered resistance. She tried but couldn't get into the Detroit Tigers' locker room. The team's general manager, Jim Campbell, told her, "Over my dead body you'll go in our Tiger clubhouse."

Robin Herman, *right*, is denied entrance to the Chicago Blackhawks locker room after a game in 1975.

But a federal court ruling in 1978 represented a major victory for female sports reporters. The groundwork was laid in 1977 when *Sports Illustrated* reporter Melissa Ludtke was denied access to the locker room during a New York Yankees playoff series. She and the magazine's parent company sued MLB commissioner Bowie Kuhn.

Ludtke filed the lawsuit because she was not given the opportunity to do her job the same as her male colleagues. The commissioner and the others claimed that keeping women out of the locker room was necessary to protect the players' privacy. A federal judge disagreed,

## LOIS FEGAN

Lois Fegan covered professional ice hockey in the 1940s for the *Harrisburg* (Pennsylvania) *Telegram*. A security guard blocked her from entering the glass-enclosed press box during a playoff game between the Hershey Bears and Cleveland Barons. She decided to improvise. She opened up her typewriter on the steps of the center aisle to work. Some of the other reporters in the press box took a vote and decided to make an exception for Fegan. She had a seat in the press box by the start of the game.

Melissa Ludtke took Major League Baseball to court over locker room access.

The Dallas Cowboys set up an interview room for all reporters to meet with players in 1978.

ruling that every reporter—male or female—must have the same access to athletes, including in locker rooms.

Some teams responded to the ruling by barring all reporters from the locker room and setting up an interview room where the media could talk with players and coaches. While that approach was fair, it caused problems for some female reporters whose male colleagues blamed them for losing the access they once had.

**Jeannie Morris, a Chicago sportscaster, had to cover an NFL game in the 1970s outside the press box during a blizzard because "the press passes said no women or children."**

But women's progress would not be slowed. By 1982 the NHL established equal access rules for its teams. The NFL and MLB did the same in 1985. And in 1987, the Association for Women in Sports Media (AWSM) was formed. Among other things, it's an organization that makes sure female journalists are treated fairly. The AWSM (pronounced "awesome") filed complaints whenever they heard that a female reporter had been denied access to a locker room.

With the help of AWSM and equal access standards, conditions improved for female sports reporters. More women would venture into the sports media world in the years that followed.

# THE AWSM WOMEN IN SPORTS

S ports journalism was once a man's world, but when women jumped onto the scene, there was no stopping them as they rose to the top.

Journalist Christine Brennan was the very first president of AWSM in 1988. Since that time she's awarded an annual scholarship at the group's conference in honor of her parents, Jim and Betty Brennan. She says she wanted to help scholarship winners move toward their own careers in sports journalism, just like she's done.

That wasn't the only "first" in Brennan's long career. She was also the first female sports reporter for the *Miami Herald* in 1981 and the first woman at the *Washington Post* to cover the local NFL team in 1985. She became an award-winning sports columnist for *USA Today* and is a television commentator, author, and public speaker. Brennan has covered every Olympics since 1984 and has broken many big stories at the Olympics, such as the 2014 Russian figure skating judging scandal.

Christine Brennan is a true pioneer in women's sports journalism.

Brennan certainly faced gender discrimination along the way. But she didn't let it stop her from doing what she wanted to do.

Another fellow member of AWSM and a female sports journalism pioneer is Lesley Visser. She paved the way for many things. Visser was the first woman to cover the World Series for a national network (1990), present the trophy to the winning Super Bowl team after working as a sideline reporter (1992), work as a regular member of the *Monday Night Football* broadcast team (1995), do color commentary for an NFL game (2001), and carry the Olympic torch during the relay to the site of the Games (2004).

Visser moved to television after writing for 14 years at the *Boston Globe*, where she covered the New England Patriots. She was the first female sports reporter at the *Globe*, too. From there, she went to work at CBS in 1987 before also adding HBO, ABC, and ESPN to her résumé. Visser was the third woman ever elected to the National Sportscasters and Sportswriters Hall of Fame and the first woman inducted in the Pro Football Hall of Fame.

Lesley Visser prepares to file a report from the sideline of an NFL playoff game in San Francisco in 1993.

# PHYLLIS GEORGE

One woman's path from the pageant stage to the sports desk was controversial. In 1975 CBS hired Phyllis George, a former Miss America, to co-host the network's highly rated *NFL Today* program on Sunday mornings. She was often criticized for her lack of journalistic experience. Critics believed that CBS hired her for her looks rather than her knowledge of sports. George remained on the *NFL Today* for parts of seven seasons between 1975 and 1984 before moving on to other projects with CBS.

ESPN calls itself the Worldwide Leader in Sports, and it has been a champion of female journalists almost from the start. ESPN began in 1979, and by 1981 Rhonda Glenn was behind the *SportsCenter* desk as its first female anchor. She often worked with Chris Berman or Tom Pipines as her co-anchors.

Glenn went on to cover women's golf for ABC Sports. She was also an amateur golfer and served as the manager of communications for the United States Golf Association.

Leandra Reilly broke into the media world after seeing how poorly women's sports were covered on her local

Phyllis George on the set of the CBS show *NFL Today* in 1976

Donna de Varona, *center*, prepares to interview runners Ruth Wysocki, *left*, and Mary Decker at the 1984 US Olympic Trials.

TV news. A job as a general assignment reporter at a TV station in Decatur, Illinois, eventually led her to Nashville, Tennessee, where she was a weekend sports anchor at the local CBS station.

Reilly went on to make history as the first woman to call the play-by-play of a National Basketball Association (NBA) game on television. She stepped into the national spotlight on February 14, 1988, when she worked a Philadelphia 76ers—New Jersey Nets game for cable outlet SportsChannel.

**Mary Carillo won the French Open mixed doubles title with John McEnroe in 1977. Her tennis career was shortened due to injury, but she thrived while broadcasting tennis and the Olympics. Carillo has won numerous honors, including two Peabody Awards for excellence in electronic media.**

For years male athletes found careers in the broadcast booth after their playing days were over. Many female athletes followed the same path. Donna de Varona was just 13 years old and the youngest member of the 1960 US Olympic swimming team when she was part of a relay team that won a gold medal. She went on to win two more gold medals in 1964 and set 18 world records in the pool.

When her athletic career ended, de Varona shifted to broadcasting with ABC and then NBC. She was the first woman in the United States to cover the Olympics on TV, working for ABC from 1972 until 1998. She specialized in commentary for swimming events. De Varona is a member of the Women's Sports Hall of Fame and won an Emmy Award in 1991.

# THE SEARCH FOR RESPECT

Gaining access to press boxes and locker rooms was a step in the right direction for women in sports media. But the fight was not over. Many women faced harassment and other unfair treatment as they tried to do their jobs.

One of the more famous female faces in the television sports world is Erin Andrews. She started out covering professional sports in Florida and Atlanta before moving on to ESPN. Andrews gained a huge following on social media as she covered numerous high-profile events. She has worked as a sideline reporter and covered the Super Bowl, MLB All-Star Game, and World Series.

In 2008 a stalker followed Andrews to different cities and filmed her through hotel room peepholes while she was dressing. The videos were posted on the Internet and viewed by millions of people. The stalker was caught and sentenced to prison while Andrews was awarded a financial settlement.

Erin Andrews leaves a Los Angeles courtroom with her attorneys in December 2009 after a man pleaded guilty to stalking her.

**Erin Andrews also won a judgment against the owner of the hotels where she was staying when she was illegally filmed. The hotel chain said it has taken steps to prevent that type of activity from happening again.**

Andrews's case certainly wasn't the first high-profile example of sexual harassment in sports media. In 1990 a locker room incident cast a shocking light on the types of on-the-job issues female reporters had to overcome. *Boston Herald* reporter Lisa Olson sued the New England Patriots and team owner Victor Kiam for sexual harassment. Olson had worked her way up from an entry-level position at the *Herald* to a role covering the city's major league teams. The 25-year-old reporter claimed that players targeted her with crude words and gestures as she waited in the locker room to talk with another player. The NFL determined that the actions of those Patriots involved were degrading to Olson. The league fined three players a total of $22,500 and the team $50,000 for the incident.

Another high-profile incident occurred on national television. Suzy Kolber had been a respected reporter who began covering the NFL and other sports at ESPN in 1993.

Lisa Olson takes part in postgame interviews in the New England Patriots locker room in 1990.

ESPN's Suzy Kolber prepares for an NFL game in 2014.

During a national broadcast of an NFL game in 2003, Kolber interviewed Pro Football Hall of Famer Joe Namath on the sideline. Twice during the live interview, Namath, who had been drinking alcohol, interrupted Kolber and told her that he wanted to kiss her. A few days later, Namath said he was embarrassed by the interview and apologized to Kolber, who accepted his apology.

Victims of harassment or sexual assault don't always come forward to share their experiences. One reason is that it can be difficult to repeat the details of the harassment in public. One reporter in particular showed great courage in sharing her story of sexual harassment.

Amelia Rayno was a sportswriter for the *Star Tribune* of Minneapolis. She covered the University of Minnesota men's basketball team. In August 2015, the university's athletic director, Norwood Teague, resigned after two school employees accused him of sexual assault. The newspaper then published Rayno's firsthand account of her experiences with Teague during her time on the beat. She shared details of how Teague harassed her and acted inappropriately toward her. Rayno's article illustrated the difficult situations that female reporters are often put in by men with whom they need to cultivate professional relationships in order to do their jobs. It's a battle that men working in sports almost never have to fight.

Inés Sainz reports from the sideline of a New York Jets game in 2010.

# INÉS SAINZ

In 2010 *Azteca* TV reporter Inés Sainz was harassed by members of the New York Jets. Sainz went to practice to interview quarterback Mark Sanchez. On the field one of the team's assistant coaches purposely overthrew footballs toward her on the practice field so he could see her jump. Half-dressed players catcalled her in the locker room later. She tweeted about her embarrassment over the players' conduct. As a result, the Jets' owner volunteered to pay for a leaguewide program to teach NFL players about sexual harassment.

Rayno wasn't the only *Star Tribune* reporter who has shared stories of workplace harassment. Rachel Blount covered the NHL's Minnesota North Stars for the newspaper in the early 1990s. After Rayno went public with her accusations against Teague, Blount tweeted that she was subjected to similar treatment by North Stars owner Norm Green. Blount said she was disheartened that her male colleagues didn't seem to think it was a problem at the time.

Harassment and unfair treatment isn't the norm for female sports journalists. But it's still a concern, much as it is for women in all fields of work.

# MORE WOMEN, MORE OPPORTUNITIES

In recent years women have taken advantage of the growing sports media landscape to carve out more opportunities to make a career in journalism.

Live television and radio sports broadcasts are still very much male-dominated. The play-by-play announcer is almost always a man, and most analysts are former players or coaches. But Beth Mowins is an exception. She joined ESPN in 1994 and has called college championships in basketball, softball, soccer, and volleyball. In 2005 she began calling college football on ESPNU. Eventually she was promoted to calling games on ESPN and ABC. She also became the second woman ever to do play-by-play for an NFL game in 2015.

Mowins was inspired to join the broadcasting ranks when she watched Phyllis George on TV. Mowins even did play-by-play in her backyard as a kid while her three brothers played games. She saw an opportunity

Beth Mowins interviews Georgetown University men's basketball coach John Thompson III.

# DORIS BURKE

Doris Burke has covered men's and women's college and professional basketball for ESPN since 1991. She says male coaches and players treat her like any other reporter and just talk basketball with her. Burke knows how much the field of sports media has changed for women during her career. According to her, the younger generation of female reporters is very prepared, polished, professional, and ready to take on careers in sports media.

with play-by-play announcing in sports because not many other women were doing it. Mowins got her start with some local and regional TV stations. She says it's important that reporters work hard to gain experience and does not think stations should put women on the air just because of their gender.

Michele Tafoya Is another woman with a long career in sports media as a broadcaster. In the mid-1990s, she hosted a talk show on the Minnesota radio station KFAN. She's also worked for CBS and NBC as a game reporter and studio host covering the NFL and college football and basketball.

Michele Tafoya, *right*, joined the NBC *Sunday Night Football* broadcast team in 2011.

Doris Burke and Dave Pasch of ESPN prepare to call the play-by-play of a men's college basketball game at New York's Madison Square Garden in 2010.

Tafoya spent a decade as a sideline reporter for *Monday Night Football*. In 2011 she joined NBC's *Sunday Night Football* team in the same role. She's worked more than 200 games on the NFL sidelines, interviewing players and

coaches during and after games. Also in 2011, she won
the Sports Emmy for Outstanding Sports Personality –
Sports Reporter.

Pam Oliver began covering the NFL for FOX Sports in 1995.

Katie Nolan used the Internet to become the face of young women in the sports media field. Nolan's witty and knowledgeable blog and videos caught the eye of executives at FOX Sports, leading to her own show, *Garbage Time*, a mix of sports commentary, comedy, and interviews with sports stars.

Sports journalism used to be exclusively a man's world. And to some extent it still is. But women have come a long way in the field. They fought and continue to fight for their right to be treated equally. A young woman who aspires to a career in sports media can get a college degree in journalism or communications, apply for jobs, and expect fair treatment. When

**Pam Oliver was a track and field All-American at Florida A&M University. She went on to a career in broadcasting and was the sideline reporter for the top FOX Sports NFL broadcast team from 1995 to 2014.**

harassment comes to light, it's not swept under the rug or considered to be part of the job anymore. Women in today's sports media have more opportunities than they've ever had in the past. With the passage of time and the efforts of talented women who refuse to remain silent in the face of discrimination, the sports media world will continue to become a more level playing field for women.

# GLOSSARY

**ACCESS**
The freedom or ability to obtain or make use of something.

**ANALYST**
In a broadcast, a person who provides details or explanations specific to the topic.

**ANCHOR**
The person who presents information during a news program.

**BEAT**
A reporter's assigned content area.

**HARASSMENT**
Intimidation or pressure from another person.

**INTERVIEW**
A conversation in which a reporter asks questions to a person involved with a story the reporter is covering.

**JOURNALIST**
A person who reports, writes, edits, or broadcasts news.

**PIONEER**
A person who was an important early figure in his or her profession.

**PLAY-BY-PLAY**
A running commentary of a sporting event.

**PRESS BOX**
An area in a stadium reserved for reporters to do their work.

## BOOKS

Cohn, Linda. *Cohn-Head: A No-Holds-Barred Account of Breaking Into the Boys' Club.* Guilford, CT: Rowman & Littlefield, 2008.

Hall, Brian. *Pioneers in Women's Sports.* Minneapolis, MN: Abdo Publishing, 2018.

Storm, Hannah, and Mark Jenkins. *Go Girl!: Raising Healthy, Confident and Successful Girls Through Sports.* Naperville, IL: Sourcebooks, Inc., 2011.

## WEBSITES

To learn more about women in sports, visit **abdobooklinks.com**. These links are routinely monitored and updated to provide the most current information available.

## PLACE TO VISIT

Newseum
555 Pennsylvania Avenue Northwest
Washington, DC 20001
202-292-6100
newseum.org
The Newseum promotes, explains, and defends the five freedoms of the First Amendment, which includes freedom of the press. The Newseum has seven levels of interactive exhibits. Learn about the history of journalism from radio and television to print and websites.

# INDEX

# ABOUT THE AUTHOR

Heather Rule is a writer, sports journalist, and social media coordinator. She earned her bachelor's degree in journalism and mass communication from the University of St. Thomas in St. Paul, Minnesota.